WHEN YOU RISE UP

53rd State Press
Brooklyn, New York

53SP 05
Published September 2009

ISBN 978-0-9817533-4-8

Library of Congress Control Number: 2009934715

53rd State Press
Brooklyn, New York

www.53rdstatepress.com

WHEN YOU RISE UP

performance texts

Miguel Gutierrez

For all of the Powerful People in my life

I could have been somebody

I could have

I could have worked with her
I could have worked with him
I could have gone there
I could have been a part of that

I could have

I could have followed him
I could have talked to them
I could have stayed
I could have waited

I could have gone for it

I could have made it happen

I could have figured it out

I could have

I think you shouldn't
I think you should
I think you shouldn't
I think you should
I think you shouldn't
I think you should
I think you shouldn't
I think you should
I think you shouldn't
I think you should
I think you shouldn't
I think you should

won't you please beat it beat it into me please
won't you please beat it beat it into me please
won't you please beat it beat it into me please
won't you please beat it beat it into me please
won't you please beat it beat it into me please
won't you please beat it beat it into me please
won't you please beat it beat it into me please

won't you please **beat** it beat it into me please
won't you please **beat** it beat it into me please
won't you please **beat** it beat it into me please
won't you please **beat** it beat it into me please
won't you please **beat** it beat it into me please
won't you please **beat** it beat it into me please
won't you please **beat** it beat it into me please

won't you please beat it beat it into me please
won't you please beat it beat it into me please
won't you please beat it beat it into me please
won't you please beat it beat it into me please
won't you please beat it beat it into me please
won't you please beat it beat it into me please
won't you please beat it beat it into me please

they're gonna find they're gonna find you somehow
they're gonna bring they're gonna bring you somehow
they're gonna take they're gonna take you somehow
they're gonna hurt they're gonna hurt you somehow

they're gonna see they're gonna see you somehow
they're gonna feel they're gonna feel you somehow
they're gonna know they're gonna know you somehow
they're gonna rip they're gonna rip you somehow

they're gonna lose they're gonna lose you somehow
they're gonna miss they're gonna miss you somehow
they're gonna love they're gonna love you somehow
they're gonna hate they're gonna hate you somehow

they're gonna pass they're gonna pass you somehow
they're gonna crush they're gonna crush you somehow
they're gonna steal they're gonna steal you somehow
they're gonna free they're gonna free you somehow

they're gonna breathe they're gonna breathe you somehow
they're gonna kill they're gonna kill you somehow
they're gonna fuck they're gonna fuck you somehow
they're gonna save they're gonna save you somehow

I am perfect and
you will love me and
everyone in this room is in this fucking dance.

you're so beautiful
you're so beautiful
i can't do this
no i can't do this
i wish we could run away together
i wish we could be perfect
i wish this could be endless
i wish we could fly
the world is such a horrible place

let's go somewhere together
let's go on a vacation together
can we plan a vacation together
can we plan one please
please
please
please
please
i wish i was more like you
i wish i was less like myself
you're so beautiful
you're like an angel
you're like a precious perfect angel
it's like a dream when i'm with you
it's like a fantasy when we're together
it's like a gorgeous gushing waterfall
perfect
you're perfect
no you're perfect
are we crazy
are we crazy
is this crazy
let's run away together
let's run far away
it'll be perfect

it'll be magic
it'll be
it'll be
it'll be like a dream
like a flower
like a rose
like a tulip
like an angel
like an angel flower tulip dream
you're my baby
no you're my baby
you're my darling
you're my darling
you're my angel
you're my angel
don't ever leave
don't ever leave me
don't ever leave me
please please
don't ever leave
don't ever leave me
don't ever leave me
please please
don't ever leave
don't ever leave me
don't ever leave me
please please

I went to the city and I realized I love you
I went to the buildings and I realized I love you
I went to the streets and I realized I love you
I went to the desert and I realized I love you
I went to the mountains and I realized I love you
I went to the cliff and I realized I love you
I went to the bridge and I realized I love you
I went to the canyon and I realized I love you
I went to the river and I realized I love you
I went to the museum and I realized I love you
I went to the wall and I realized I love you
I went to the toilet and I realized I love you
I went to the bookstore and I realized I love you
I went to the wind and I realized I love you
I went to the clouds and I realized I love you
I went to the moon and I realized I love you
I went to the sunrise and I realized I love you
I went to the end and I realized I love you

I went to my face and I realized I love you
I went to my eyes and I realized I love you
I went to my mouth and I realized I love you
I went to my lips and I realized I love you
I went to my tongue and I realized I love you
I went to my neck and I realized I love you
I went to my chest and I realized I love you
I went to my arms and I realized I love you
I went to my hands and I realized I love you
I went to my dick and I realized I love you
I went to my ass and I realized I love you
I went to my legs and I realized I love you
I went to my feet and I realized I love you
I went to my toes and I realized I love you
I went to my bed and I realized I love you
I went to my dreams and I realized I love you

I went into the store and decided to buy peaches.

It was an unfamiliar feeling, because I don't normally go into that store, don't normally buy peaches, and it's a little bit out of the way.

I wondered if I should get some for my friends. They like peaches, and I don't usually get them presents for no reason.

I decided against it. They're too heavy, and I really should only buy the things that I need today.

So I went on with my day.

I saw a kid on the street. I saw him crying, and I saw his father grab him by the wrist and say stop that shit. Just stop it. I thought he was going to hit the kid, and heard myself thinking,

Please don't.

He didn't. He didn't do it because it didn't happen. I made it up. I thought it would sound meaningful. Important.

But I did walk down the street and I did see things that I didn't like and I did hear myself saying,

You can't say anything.
Not now.
Keep your mouth shut.

Just then my father called and I decided for once to answer the phone. He said Mijito. Porque no nos has llamado? Why haven't you called us?

And I stuttered and I tried to think of something to say and I changed the subject.

I talked about the weather.
I talked about rehearsals.
I talked about my IRS audit.
I talked about my friends.
I talked about the war.
I talked about the weekend.

No I didn't. I didn't talk about it. I didn't talk about the war. Why did I say that I did? Why did I say that I did? Why did I say that I did that I did.
Why did I say that I did that I did.
Why did I say that I did that I did.
Why did I say that I did that I did.
I'm so confused. I told my dad, Dad, you're interrupting me. You're interrupting me and you're interrupting my monologue. You're always interrupting.

I stopped at a pizzeria. I sat down next to two women who were talking about the meaning of the word crescendo. INXS was playing on the radio:

Devil inside,
the devil inside,
every single one of us the devil inside.

I thought about Michael Hutchence in his final moments, the belt around his neck and his dick in his hand. I thought about that awful television show where they auditioned a new lead singer for INXS. Ten years after the fact and anyway, who the fuck cares about INXS anymore.

I took the train home. I saw a woman I know sitting across from me. I did that thing you do where you see someone you know but you pretend you haven't seen them. I looked down at my shoes, acted like I was lost in thought, in my very active imagination. I thought about how she was pretending too, how she knew I was there and how <u>we</u> were so close to each other.

I looked up at the advertisement above her head. It read:

Nothing shines like brick.

I got home and sat on the toilet <u>and</u> turned the shower on, because the sound of running water is my favorite sound in the world. I opened my book and continued to read from where I'd left off. This is what I read:

The speed of technology makes the world a smaller and thus more claustrophobic, place.
I believe that there will be for future generations, a feeling of confinement in the world, of incarceration, which will certainly be at the limit of tolerability, by virtue of the speed of information...
How do we not become so immobilized by the presence of the present all around us, either from the Web, or this constant terrible connectedness that comes from everything from cell phones to IMs to e-mails?

I read that and got all excited inside. I continued to sit on the toilet <u>and</u> muttered to myself a little bit. I flushed the toilet again <u>and</u> waited for it to refill.

In my room, the phone rang. <u>It was my friend.</u>

I said, what's going on? He said Real Estate.

Real estate real estate real estate real estate.

My head hurt a little bit. I wasn't quite sure what to say. I heard myself saying.

uh huh.

uh huh.

I thought about all of the silence on the phone and my voice digitizing its way through the air.

You're saying uhhuh uhhuh said my friend.

I said No, I'm listening. I just don't know what to say. It sounds stressful.

It's true. I don't own anything really. Nothing expensive besides my computer. I didn't know what to say.

I laid down. The stoplight from the street made shadows and stripes of color along the wall and the ceiling. Green, then yellow, then red. The changes were soft. Silent. I thought if I made a movie this is what I'd film. Myself in this bed, looking at the wall, my body floating on this ship of a mattress.

Cars went by and I could hear the whirring of the fan in my room.

I went to sleep. I dreamed about murder and break-ins and horrible things I don't normally dream about. I dreamed I was having sex with my ex-boyfriend and it was scary and real, and then he was having sex with other people and looking at me. I woke myself up, feeling sick.

It was late. I had slept in again. The curtain was pinned to the sill to block out the sunlight. I'm in this room. I will always wake up in this room.

I walked into the living room. It was dark. I went to the computer and opened it up and went to the front page of the newspaper.

There was an article that said 600,000 Iraqi people have died so far. The study has a margin of error that ranges from 426,369, to 793,663 deaths. I looked at that number.

I thought, Oh no. Don't write that. You aren't really going to say that. That's dumb. That's didactic. Theater is a space of imagination.

I came back into my room, shut the door and wrote this all down.

When you rise up, you must sing songs

The leaves are changing color again
My heart is broken. BREAKING!
      I   don't
      know
      anything
You're so far away
What is this distance
Why won't you
Why won't you
Why won't you come closer
This is how a piece ends
We stop orrr
We leave orrr
We confuse you orrr –
I wonder
I wonder what it will take for any of this to matter
sometimes it seems like a dream
that any of this happened
that you were there & I was here
we were
we were in the same place
Oh
Oh
Oh how many bad poems will I write this year
ten?
ten twenty?
two hundred twenty?
everybody's got one,
      two,
      three plus ways of looking at things
What is my way.
bottoms up.
I look up at you.

You are so much bigger than me.
Ohhhhh
Ohhhhh
Ohhhhh
Oh I am just this boy.
This something I don't understand.
Really.
I am becoming more and more something that is not
me.
it's a joke
really
how the air
comes in
and out
of
my body
makes
me move
all
all i see
ALL I SEE IS WINTER
A dumpster in front of my house
waiting like
waiting like a dirty pool
an above ground coffin
can i swim in it?
can i swim in it?
with the
candy
wrappers
          and the
plastic
bags
          and the

everything
we don't want
that tell you a story
a story of excess.
I am
I am
I am a piece of onion paper
transparent
brittle
write on me & smudge the words OH!
so that I might feel something
something.
something.
something.
running
I am running
I am running down the driveway
I am running
running to catch you
To catch you before you go
The wind is blowing in our faces
The dust from the road is choking me
choking me
I have to tell you
I have to tell you this thing
This might be my only chance
My only chance to tell you
I am filled
I am filled with so much emotion for you
Can you feel it?
Can you feel it too?
I am squeezing your arm.
Your arm is squeezing me back.

We are connected.
I am not letting it go.
The emotion is going from me
into you now.
This is why we are together.
Why we have spent this time this way.
I had to
I had to
I had to tell you.
I needed you to know before you left.
This is the last piece that I make for you.
This is the last piece that will
look like
feel like
sound like
smell like this.
It's not –
It's something –
It's not
It's un
It's not
It's something
I needed you to know before you left.
It's not –
It's something –
It's not
It's un
It's not
It's something
I needed you to know before you left.
It's not
It's un
It's not
It's something

It's not
It's un
It's not
It's unrealistic
No.
I can't
No.
I can't imagine it.
No.
I can't imagine it at all.
No.
The sun is outside.
No.
The sun is outside.
No.
Are you
No.
Are you writing a po-em?
Yes.
Are you?
No.
Are you writing a poem?
Yes.
Yes I am.
Yes I am writing a poem.
One down
One down
One down
One down
One down
One down
One down
One down
One down

One down
One down
One down
One down
One down
One down
One down
One down
One down
One down

So
         many
more
to go.

I dreamed I was beautiful.
I dreamed it
and
It felt real
and I felt
everyone's eyes looking at me with pleasure
as I passed.
I was an object of curiosity.
Still
but shiny, glowing.
something you wanted to touch or possess even.
I dreamed I was beautiful
and that
the whole world smiled in my direction
saying yesss
yesss we're glad you're here
thank you for giving us something to look up to
something better than we are.
It was so perfect.
So perfectly right that I was so beautiful.
Like everyone agreeing on the obvious solution
nodding in unison at what was of course, the truth.

I dreamed I was beautiful
perfect
a fantastic artist
brilliant
I had ideas and they were all great and
everybody loved my work

I dreamed you were burning
you were burning
down to the very earth of you
we went to bed to fuck and your
skin cracked off you and
fell to the floor
like autumn leaves

I dreamed I was beautiful
but it didn't matter
you left anyway and I
reached out to your grizzled
hand as it swung behind you with
all the confidence of someone really
going somewhere and my outreach was this
long horizontal song of grief
no no no no

Oh my my my my my
Oh my my my my my
Once upon a time
It was beautiful here
and the sun came and set fire to the ground
until it was black, scorched and hard
There was nothing
nothing
nothing left for us here

Once upon a time
It was beautiful here
and the prince let down his guard
you should have seen it
flowers falling from his chest his
hands, collapsing to the ground and
baring the whole front of his insides open
glistening and shiny

I can't tell you what to add on
what's not to add
memories are my little fictions
covering me with feathers

Some people will say this looks like bleh
Some people will say this sounds like bluh
But this is my piece,
My piece my piece MY piece

The Problem With Dancing

It doesn't sell
It doesn't last
It doesn't mean anything
It doesn't translate well
It doesn't make you rich
It doesn't keep you warm at night
It doesn't dance enough
It doesn't make the ones who aren't dancing dance
It doesn't move product
It doesn't sell papers
It doesn't cure cancer
It doesn't cure AIDS

It doesn't stop global warming
It doesn't recycle
It doesn't impeach presidents
It doesn't stop war
It doesn't house the refugees
It doesn't get you a visa
It doesn't re-unite your family
It doesn't impress them when you're fat
It doesn't pay for maternity leave

It doesn't get you noticed
It doesn't get you laid
It doesn't fuck like a 25 year old
It doesn't bring your ex back he's never coming back

It doesn't wreck homes
It doesn't get you married
It doesn't hold up next to movies
It doesn't hold up next to music
It doesn't open galleries
It doesn't please your parents
It doesn't make sense to go to college for it
It doesn't change if you go to college for it
>   If you see something say something (something)
>   If you see something say something (something)
>   Say, say, say what you want
>   But DONT PLAY GAMES WITH MY AFFECTION

It doesn't pay the rent
It doesn't buy you a house
It doesn't have a mortgage
It doesn't look as hard as it is
It doesn't matter unless it's hard
It doesn't have be to be hard to be good
It doesn't tell you it's good

It doesn't get the aisle seat
It doesn't have a metrocard
It doesn't clear your wrinkles
It doesn't clear your acne
It doesn't resolve the problems with your combination skin
It doesn't do layaway
It doesn't shine your shoes
It doesn't lick your boots
It doesn't shine your shoes
>   Salmivaara, Salmivaara
>   Wan Tu
>   Salmivaara (2x)
>   Wadalatee Wa-ah!
>   Wadalatee Wa-ah! (2x)

It doesn't get written about well
It doesn't remember itself
It doesn't come cheap
It doesn't happen anywhere
It doesn't say I love you
It doesn't last long
It doesn't end soon enough
It doesn't stop hurting
It doesn't age well
It doesn't say I'm sorry

Kiss suck fuck cum
Kiss suck fuck cum

Oh, yeah, oh! Put it in there
Oh, yeah, oh! Put it in there
Fuck that hole
Fuck that hole
Fuck that hole

Oh, yeah, oh! Put it in there
Oh, yeah, oh! Put it in there
Fuck that hole
Fuck that hole
Fuck that hole

Fuck that hole	Oh, yeah, oh!
Fuck that hole	Put it in there
Fuck that hole	Oh, yeah, oh!
Fuck that hole	Put it in there

Fuck that hole
Fuck that hole
Fuck that hole

You like getting that big fat cock sucked?

You like getting that big fat cock sucked?

Oh! oh oh oh Oh! I'm cumming
Oh! oh oh oh Oh! I'm cumming

You like getting that big fat cock sucked?
You like getting that big fat cock sucked?

Oh! oh oh oh Oh! I'm cumming
Oh! oh oh oh Oh! I'm cumming

I'm cumming, I'm cumming, I'm cumming
I'm cumming, I'm cumming, I'm cumming on your
FACCCCCCCCE-ah

It doesn't stop genocide
It doesn't raise the water levels
It doesn't have health care
It doesn't stop corruption
It doesn't stop paybacks
It doesn't stop dictators
It doesn't re-constitute the power of the constitution

MY ISSUES MY WEATHER MY STORIES
MY NEIGHBORHOOD MY NEWS!!

It doesn't punish george bush for war crimes
It doesn't bring the soldiers back
It doesn't separate church from state
It doesn't stop riots
It doesn't start riots

It doesn't have corporate sponsors
It doesn't have the right space
It doesn't have the right funding
It doesn't have the right audience

It doesn't have the right theater
It doesn't get the right response

    OH ANN LIV!
    OH ANN LIV COME BAAAACK!
    OH ANN LIV DON'T GET LOST!
    OH J.!
    OH J. COME BACK!
    OH J. DON'T GET LOST!

It doesn't do email
It doesn't fill stadiums
It looks stupid on youtube
It looks stupider on myspace which just sends you to
youtube
It doesn't sell magazines
It doesn't make millions
It doesn't do coffee
It doesn't speak to the people
It doesn't integrate the poor

    I dreamed I was beautiful.
    I dreamed it
    and
    It felt real
    and I felt
    everyone's eyes looking at me with pleasure
    as I passed.
    I was an object of curiosity.
    Still
    but shiny, glowing.
    something you wanted to touch or possess even.
    I dreamed I was beautiful
    and that
    the whole world smiled in my direction
    saying yesss
    yesss we're glad you're here
    thank you for giving us something to look up to

something better than we are.
It was so perfect.
So perfectly right that I was so beautiful.
Like everyone agreeing on the obvious solution
nodding in unison at what was of course, the truth.
It doesn't end the legacy of slavery
It doesn't end the legacy of colonialism
It doesn't save the Native Americans
It doesn't stop the shootings
It doesn't save the whales
It doesn't stop the poseurs
It doesn't house the homeless
It doesn't stop rape
It doesn't stop domestic abuse
It doesn't stop people from using the rite of spring

It doesn't grow up
It doesn't look good on a wall
It doesn't photograph well
It doesn't keep those dumb people from saying "oh my god, when are you gonna come over and watch project runway" goddammit

It doesn't keep your hair in place
It doesn't rebuild Iraq
It doesn't do lunch
It doesn't have a business card
It doesn't sell stocks
It doesn't fit in your ipod

It doesn't have a chance
It doesn't work in specific sites
It doesn't like definitions
It doesn't stop getting made fun of
It doesn't look normal

It doesn't pay for your per diem
It doesn't pay for your flight

It doesn't costume easily
It doesn't let you leave
It doesn't stop feeling good
It doesn't stop coming
It doesn't stop coming
It doesn't stop coming
It doesn't stop coming
It doesn't stop coming
It doesn't stop coming
It doesn't stop coming
It doesn't stop coming

That is the problem with dancing!
That is the problem with dancing
That is the problem with dancing!
That is the problem with dancing

how to be an artist

you are born to parents who don't know really how to deal with you. they leave the house and you go up to your mother's make up table and adorn yourself in powders, colors, smears of spectacular hues which convince you that you are, in fact, beautiful. you carefully try to remember where all of the instruments of fantasy were before you boy-handled them. inevitably you forget and return things to the wrong place and your mother, later, noticing the differences, stands alone by the table, stares at the misplaced lipstick and wonders how things got to this point and how will she keep this (yet another) secret from your father.

you beg, lie, cheat or steal your way into some kind of situation where you can be taught SOMETHING by another person/mentor/artist/hapless fuck who has ended up teaching a greedy little know-it-all like you.

you go to a school where the other children vacation on the weekends and summers in homes far away from yours. you become like them but you are not quite like them but you are enough like them to be thought of being like them. you have convinced yourself of this as well and so it goes. you have learned how to learn what clothes to wear, what products to buy, what jokes to make – just how many and in what tone of voice. later you will travel all around the world and as if by instinct, or the smell of the air, you will find a way to consort with others who are like you. you will try and tell yourself that you are having interesting, different "experiences," but in fact you are repeating the same pattern of aping and personality morphing that you learned when you were very very young.

you are invited to large institutions in minor cities where children walk around in clumps and lines wearing scarves and furry boots. you are handed all manners of metal and plastic, some of which enter into doorknobs and some of which slide through cracks in plastic boxes. doors pop open and close according to the command of the talismans. doors to garages, buildings, rooms, cabinets. everything is about getting IN or keeping something OUT. a stereo waits in neutralized silence before you open the door to it and send power running through its synapses. a chair waits in early morning shadow for you to arrive and to sit on it. everything, it seems, is waiting everywhere for you to arrive and to give it a reason, though you doubt that it's that simple.

you find yourself in front of large numbers of children at these institutions, barking out orders and making shapes that they, in turn, imitate. every now and then you stop and look at their taut, unworn faces. you explain things and they nod, as if they understand or care but neither is true because how could they really? you secretly want to tell them: get out, go far away from this dumb place or its ossified patterns might make permanent residence in your bloodstream. but you don't say this. you soldier on with the barking and the shapes.

you look at the boys in these gatherings at these institutions. you look at their slim, agile bodies as if you were looking at a foreign animal in a zoo. where do these boys come from? why are there so many of them? you feel the distance between yourself and them widening. maybe it was always this way. it seems impossible that you were ever this young, that your own body was ever this uncomplicated. you find ways of placing your hands on them (it is part of your job) and they feel strong, warm, with rounded muscles that lengthen or slide smooth over themselves. it's like you're touching aliens from another world and you hate them and you hate yourself and you hate them.

you create things – things that have little discernible value other than to you and to a select group of people who have convinced themselves that these worthless things also have value. you create these things mostly so that these people know your name, and so that they repeat it to others when you are not around. you hope that this game of name uttering – much like a phone tree – will continue uninterrupted for as long as you live and then way beyond that. you hope that at some point someone will write the name (your name) down in newspapers and, better, books. you characterize your efforts to yourself as "research," "exploration," your "body of work," but really it's this name thing that you're concerned about.

but this thing, yes, this thing of no value. you give it away repeatedly, in front of many people whose eyes follow your actions like a tennis match. you wonder why you give it away. it's so private really. you give it with all of your heart, the way you felt when you were little and you were home alone and the music was on. you give it away like this but it doesn't matter. they don't really want it anyway. it's so fragile, like a soap bubble. the thing is as momentary and inconsequential as that. all it takes is the vibration of a cell phone or a baby's cry for it to fall apart. wanting attention for this worthless thing just feels greedy and childish.

you are invited by other people (who, incidentally, like to have their name known as well) to audition this thing that you created to other people, who may or may not end up remembering, liking or saying your name. you are excited but you suspect that maybe this is, as they say, a "mixed blessing." you travel and find yourself in these gatherings of similarly conflicted souls. you and the other souls walk around in a daze. should you talk to each other? should you actually ask each other questions? maybe it's dangerous to talk. maybe something will happen to you that you can't control if you talk. maybe you will give something away that you won't be able to get back later. maybe it's better for you just to sit at separate tables and make fleeting glances at each other as if you were cruising on a train.

you travel to these gatherings in enormous sardine cans which, impossibly, fly through clouds, and in which there isn't enough air and where everyone seems to be screaming or suffocating. while in the sardine can you busy yourself with any number of heretofore unimagined lines of private exploration – can you fart into a cloth covered seat without it being heard or smelled? can you learn the names and latitudinal co-ordinates of all the cities in eastern europe? can you masturbate quickly in a bathroom the size of a coffin and emerge looking as if nothing has happened?

you lie awake at night in beds in foreign countries, hearing the muddy voices of passing revelers on the streets outside your window. you lie naked, gently stroking your penis like it's a sleeping pet, or the hair of a lover who's fallen asleep in your lap. you try to remember someone you fucked once. you conjure the image of this person astride your body or astride a new lover's body. maybe you dream about everyone you ever fucked and you flutter through images of ex-es like a flip book, creating a film of desire and conquest, forever suspended in the time you spent in other people's bedrooms. you hope for some kind of response or excitement to begin in your crotch. maybe this warmth will expand outwards into the rest of your dispassionate body. maybe it will be a moment of heat in your day, a moment not driven by indecision or doubt.

you wake up confused, depressed, wondering how this day will turn out. you have no plan, no REAL concept of why you have woken up, no real concept of why you should actually DO anything at all. your curiosity for living and creating is only matched by your deeply held belief that none of it matters. in some cases this latter feeling far outweighs the former.

you want lovers, or you think you want lovers. lovers in every port. it sounds like a good idea maybe. lovers in other cities will offer you uncomplicated romantic interactions charged with non stop erotic excitement. but the truth of it is is that most sex leaves you uninspired and most people seem too far away even when they're inside of you. you fall in love (maybe) sometimes with others whose alleged likeness to you makes you think that there could be hope – a "new life" – far from your actual life, in some charming corner of the world far away from your small, squalid and depressing apartment.

you think to yourself: how terrible, how utterly unfair that this fate has befallen you, when someone so much more deserving, more intelligent, more talented could have ended up with this life. someone who would appreciate it more, read up on the local history, learn a few of the words. no, it has fallen to you, you who are so deeply uncurious about the ideas of others. you, who just wish to sleep and to watch television. you, who walk around the different cities of the world with nary a hint of why things look the way they look. you, who only listen to the polyphony of sensation and judgment ever present in your body and mind. you, who feel that, in a way, any experience is like any other, with only lesser or greater disappointment articulating the difference. you, who only ever wish to know about your own thoughts, your own ideas about the ways things are or should be. you. you shudder to yourself when you realize that this is how you feel. you feel guilty for it, maybe a little bit ashamed. but that shame quickly subsides the next time you go on an extended hay ride through your imagination, enamored of every little idea you manage to concoct.

"I could have..." and "won't you please..." from *Retrospective Exhibitionist*, "I am perfect..." from *Difficult Bodies*, premiered November 30, 2005 in NY at Dance Theater Workshop. *Difficult Bodies* originally performed by Anna Azrieli, Michelle Boulé and Abby Crain

"you're so beautiful" and "i went to the city..." from *myendlesslove*, premiered November 11, 2006 at in NY at MIX: The NY Gay and Lesbian Experimental Film and Video Festival.

"I went to the store..." (Group Monologue), "When you rise up" and "The leaves are changing color" (Michelle's monologue) from *Everyone*, premiered March 1, 2007 in NY at Abrons Art Center in co-presentation with Danspace Project's Out of Space Program. Group Monologue contains excerpts from "The Devil Inside," written by Michael Hutchence and Andrew Farriss, and quotes from Paul Virilio and Steve Kurtz, from Creative Time's Who Cares. *Everyone* originally performed by: Anna Azrieli, Michelle Boulé, Abby Crain, Chris Forsyth, Miguel Gutierrez, Isabel Lewis, Daniel Linehan, Otto Ramstad, Elizabeth Ward

"I dreamed I was beautiful" (1st 2nd and 3rd) and "Oh my...." from the I HATE OUTSIDE section of *Brindabella*, a piece created by Philip Adams that I was commissioned to create a section of. Premiered in Melbourne, Australia, December 5, 2007 at the Malthouse Theater. Performed by Derrick Amanatidis, Luke George, Tim Harvey, Kyle Kremerskothen, Brooke Stamp

The Problem With Dancing, first version performed in Durham, North Carolina, at American Dance Festival's Faculty Concert, July 15, 2007 in Page Auditorium. Includes lyrics from "Say Say Say," by Michael Jackson and Paul McCartney and ad copy from subway ads. Performed by Andrew Champlin and Miguel Gutierrez

"how to be an artist" from *Nothing, No thing*, premiered May 23, 2008 in NY at LaMaMa.

Thanks to Anna Azrieli, Michelle Boulé, Abby Crain, Chris Forsyth, Daniel Linehan, Isabel Lewis, Otto Ramstad, Elizabeth Ward, Andrew Champlin, Derrick Amanatidis, Luke George, Tim Harvey, Kyle Kremerskothen and Brooke Stamp for speaking some of these words and for giving me a reason to write them.

Thanks to Cathy Edwards, Stephen Kent Jusick, Jay Wegman, Laurie Uprichard, Phillip Adams, Donna Faye Burchfield, Nicky Paraiso and Mia Yoo for giving me gigs to write them for. Thanks to Marissa Perel for encouragement. Thanks to Karinne Keithley and 53rd State Press for the chance to get it together. Thanks to Ben Pryor for all of the sass.

Miguel Gutierrez is a Brooklyn based dance and music artist. He creates group work in collaboration with dancers, visual and music artists as the director of Miguel Gutierrez and the Powerful People, and he also makes solos. He has created several full evenings of work that have been presented internationally in venues such as Dance Theater Workshop in New York, the Walker Art Center in Minneapolis and ImPulsTanz in Vienna. He was the instigator of freedom of information, a performance/protest/meditation project in 2001 and 2008. He has received support from the NEA, Jerome Foundation, Creative Capital, Rockefeller MAP Fund, New York Foundation for the Arts. He has two New York Dance and Performance "Bessie" Awards: for dancing with John Jasperse Company, and for choreography. As a singer, he has performed with My Robot Friend, Antony and the Johnsons and Vincent Segal. He teaches classes regularly around the world and he invented DEEP (Death Electric Emo Protest) AEROBICS. www.miguelgutierrez.org

Book design: Karinne Keithley
Photos: Alex Escalante
from *Everyone*
(L to R: Daniel Linehan, Isabel Lewis, Michelle Boulé)

53rd State Press publishes new plays and performance texts. It was founded in 2007 by Karinne Keithley.

For more information, please visit 53rd State Press at www.53rdstatepress.org

To learn more about Miguel Gutierrez, visit www.miguelgutierrez.org

53SP 01 The Book of the Dog
53SP 02 Joyce Cho Plays
53SP 03 Nature Theater of Oklahoma's No Dice
53SP 04 Nature Theater of Oklahoma's Rambo Solo
53SP 05 When You Rise Up
53SP 06 Montgomery Park, or Opulence

Forthcoming 2009-10:
new plays by Sibyl Kempson